MW00575419

GOD MADE BABIES

Helping Parents Answer the Baby Question

Justin S. Holcomb &
Lindsey A. Holcomb

Illustrated by
Trish Mahoney

God blessed them and said to them,
"Be fruitful and multiply and fill the earth."

Genesis 1:28

Dear Parent or Caregiver,

"Where do babies come from?" You can count on, at some point, being asked this question by your child. Preparing ahead of time can help make conversations more casual, more natural, and consequently, more effective.

Children ask: "Where do babies come from?" because they are curious. Their question is not about sex. They want to know where *they* came from before they were born. The question is a healthy and normal part of a child's development. Many children around the age of three or four start to notice pregnant women, which then sparks their curiosity and questions. Children can understand that reproduction is a natural part of life, and that God made all living things to reproduce.

This book is not "The Talk" and is not intended to replace your conversations with your child. Rather it is meant to be a resource to help start those conversations. Please don't think that this topic will be a one-time conversation that you never revisit. Your goal is to create an atmosphere that encourages question asking and answering on the part of both you and your child.

This is a wonderful opportunity for you to become their main source for this information. Being open, safe, available, and prepared when they want to talk is very important. This book aims to help you answer their questions in an honest, biblical, and age-appropriate way. As you read this book with your children, you will be able to ground your conversation in how God created his world and how he created them. You will want to keep reminding your children that every baby is a gift from God and that they are God's special gift to you. Enjoy reading and enjoy helping your children understand more about our amazing God and how he makes all things!

Thank you for taking the time to read this book and talk with your child about it.

Best,
Lindsey Holcomb, MPH
Justin Holcomb, PhD

God likes to make things.
Because God is creative, he likes to

CREATE.

And God likes making all sorts of things!

Big things. Small things. Fast things. Slow things.
Hot things. Cold things. Wet things. Dry things.

God made flying, spinning, growing, swimming, crawling,
squirming, jumping, sleeping, and walking things.

In the beginning, God made the heavens and the earth.

He made the entire universe and filled it with the sun, the moon, stars, and planets.

The universe is absolutely huge and contains galaxies and solar systems. Humans do not even know how large the universe is because it is too big for us to measure.

But God knows how big it is.

God made all things by his creative and powerful words.
He made everything because God likes to create.

God made sky and sea and filled them with birds and
sea creatures. He made green parrots and pink flamingos.
He made night owls and early birds.

He made penguins who live in icy cold places.
And he made eagles who soar in the mountains.
God made small starfish and big whales.
He made fast sharks and slow jellyfish.

God made land and filled it with plants, trees, animals, and humans.

Plants and trees make oxygen for us to breathe and some make fruits and vegetables that we eat.

Some animals—like monkeys—have fur.
Some animals—like lions—make loud noises.

God made people in many different colors, shapes, and sizes.
He loves to create.
God was so excited to make you!

ROAR!

God likes making things so much that he made living things able to make more things like themselves.

The word for this is
"reproduction."

God made living things that can make offspring. It means that God's creatures can join him in making other creatures like themselves.

To the sea creatures and birds, God said,
"Be fruitful and multiply and fill the waters in the seas,
and let birds multiply on the earth."*

To humans, God said,
"Be fruitful and multiply and fill the earth."†

God made his creatures to be able to
make more creatures like themselves.
He did this on purpose as a wonderful gift.

* Genesis 1:22
† Genesis 1:28

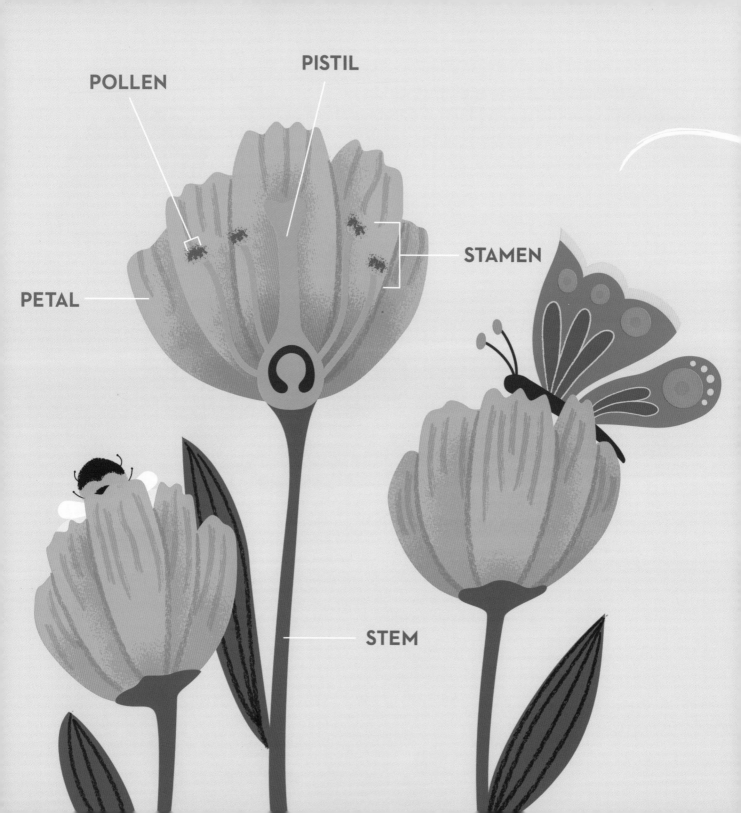

POLLEN

PISTIL

PETAL

STAMEN

STEM

God made flowers.
And he made flowers so they can make more flowers.

Flowers make nectar and pollen.
Nectar is a sugary liquid and pollen is a fine powder that is
usually yellow and sometimes makes you sneeze.
Pollen is from the male part of one flower called the stamen.
Pollen makes seeds by spreading to the female part
of another flower, called the pistil.

Pollen can't move by itself and needs helpers.
Animal helpers come to the flower to drink the nectar.
They get a sweet drink, and the plant pollen gets stuck to the animal.
When the animal moves on to another flower, the pollen goes with it and
then sticks to the pistil. When this happens, the flower makes seeds,
which make new flowers.

Bees, birds, bats, butterflies, beetles, and ladybugs are very
important helpers that move pollen to help make new flowers.

Isn't it amazing how God makes new flowers?

God made some animals to make babies by laying eggs.
Birds, fish, reptiles, insects, turtles, and lizards are some
of the animals whose babies come from eggs.

Do you remember how it takes two
flowers to make new flowers?
It also takes two animals to make
babies that come from eggs.

Most snakes come from eggs.

A mom snake lays eggs on the ground, and then the mom
and dad snakes coil around them to keep them safe.

Mom frogs lay their eggs in the water and mom sea turtles lay their eggs in holes they dig on the beach.

Most birds lay their eggs in a nest.

The mom and dad birds sit on them to keep them warm while the babies grow in the eggs. It takes a few weeks for the bird eggs to hatch. "Hatching" is when the baby animal comes out of the egg.

God made some animals that carry their babies inside the mom.

Animals like this include
dogs, cats, bears, cows, and deer,
just to name a few.

These animals are called
mammals.

Some animals reproduce by giving birth to young ones.
Just like it takes two animals to make babies that come from eggs,
it also takes two animals to make baby mammals,
which do not come from eggs,
like puppies, kittens, cubs, calves, and fawns.

Some animals, like cows, usually have only one baby
in the mom at a time. Other animals, like dogs, may have
six or more babies in the mom at the same time.

God made people and made them in his image.
We were created by God, for God,
to be like God, and to be with God.

That makes each of us extra special!
God made us able to make babies that
would grow up and make more people.
That's what it means to "be fruitful and multiply."

It takes two people to make a baby.
You need two parts to make a baby—
a small part from the dad and
a small part from the mom.

A sperm from the dad and an egg from the mom join together in the mom's body. The baby grows in a special sac called the uterus. Another word for this is womb.

Each baby
is a
GIFT
from
GOD!

A baby grows inside the mom for about **9** months.

A baby's heart starts beating when she or he has been in the mom for just four weeks. This is also when the baby's brain begins growing and the baby's arms, legs, eyes, and ears begin to form.

HEART

4
weeks

LUNGS

All the most important parts of a baby—their heart, lungs, kidneys, and intestines—are fully formed at 10 weeks. At this time, they also have fingers, toes, and eyelids. Babies even have fingerprints!

The baby's bones and muscles grow stronger and stronger until it is time to be born.

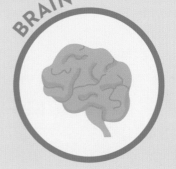

BRAIN

POPPYSEED

4 weeks: The baby is the size of a poppyseed

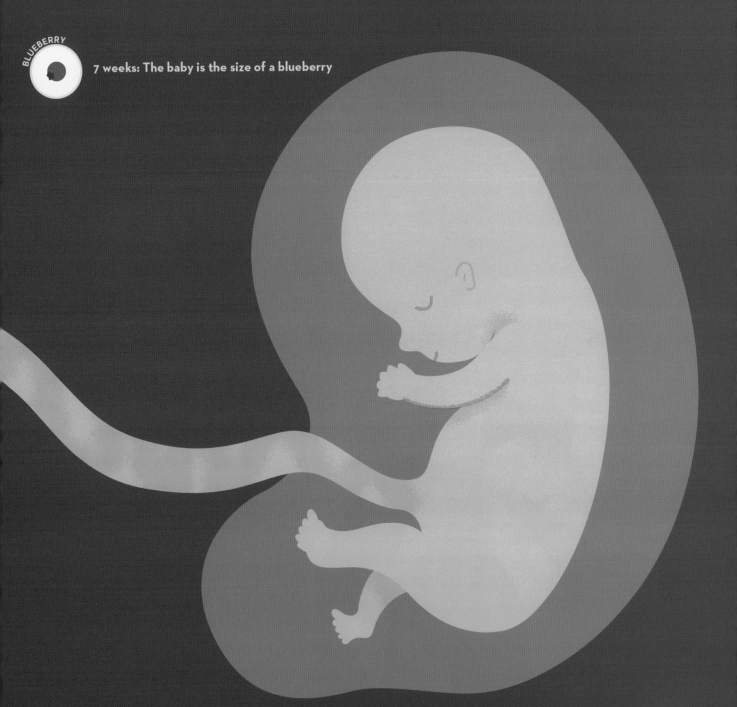

BLUEBERRY

7 weeks: The baby is the size of a blueberry

STRAWBERRY

10 weeks: The baby is the size of a strawberry

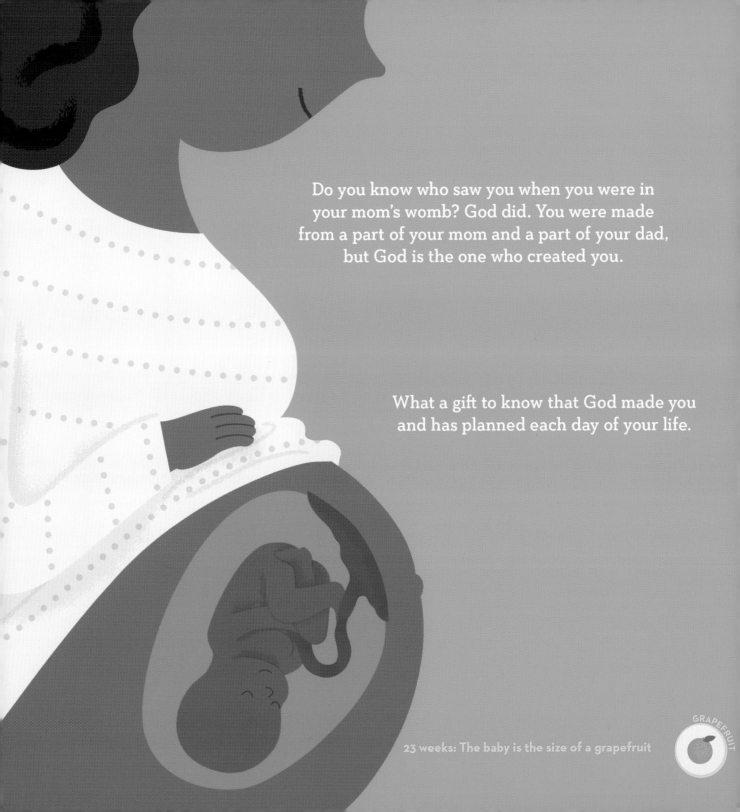

Do you know who saw you when you were in your mom's womb? God did. You were made from a part of your mom and a part of your dad, but God is the one who created you.

What a gift to know that God made you and has planned each day of your life.

23 weeks: The baby is the size of a grapefruit

GRAPEFRUIT

PINEAPPLE

For you created my inmost being; you knit me together in my mother's womb.

I praise you because I am

fearfully and

wonderfully made;

your works are wonderful, I know that full well.

My frame was not hidden from you when I was made in the secret place, when I was woven together in the depths of the earth. Your eyes saw my unformed body; all the days ordained for me were written in your book before one of them came to be.*

* Psalm 139:13–16 NIV

What do babies do inside the mom?

While babies grow in the mom,
they are very active.

Just like children and grown-ups, babies need to eat.
To help them grow, babies get their food through a tube
that is connected to the mom. This is how they eat.
This tube is why you have a belly button.

While inside their mom, babies also sleep, kick their feet, blink, smile, and even suck their thumbs!

They like to move around because babies have new muscles and want to use them.

Babies can hear from inside their mom's body, and sometimes they get the hiccups.

Babies grow **bigger** and **bigger** until they are ready to be born and come out of the mom's body.

How does the baby get out
of the mom's body?

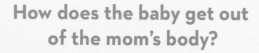

God thought of everything.
He designed the mom's body so that
when the baby is ready to be born, the
mom's body lets the baby out.

After the baby grows bigger and bigger for nine
months in the mom, the muscles in the uterus
gently push the baby out through the
vagina. Sometimes a doctor may make
a small cut in the mom's belly so
the baby can come out that way.

Everyone is so **HAPPY** when they see the **BABY!**

"Children are a gift from the Lord."*

Because God says children are a gift from him,
sometimes children ask very good questions.

Girls may wonder,

Can I have a baby grow
inside me too?

Boys may wonder,

Can I help make a baby?

Only a grown-up woman can
grow a baby inside her.
And only a grown-up man can
help make a baby.

* Psalm 127:3 NIrV

When you grow up, you can have children of your own. Being a mom or dad is a big responsibility and brings lots of joy.

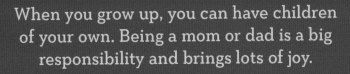

Between now and when you might be a parent, **there are lots of important things for you to learn so you can take care of a baby.**

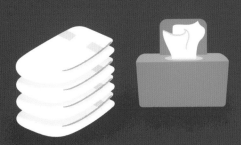

Did you know that long ago—before time even began—
God planned for you to be here?

God made you on purpose because he wanted you in his world.

God knew your hair and eye color even before you were born. Jesus said,
"Even the hairs on your head are all numbered."*

God knew if you'd be a girl or a boy.
He knew what gifts and abilities you would have too.

God knew all about you and was excited for you to be born!

The Bible says that God put you exactly where he
wants you so you can seek him and know him.†

†See Acts 17:26–27

Things to Consider When Asked the
BABY QUESTION

Our goal is to help you answer the question: "Where do babies come from?" The younger the child, the less detail they need.

The answer many young children can understand clearly is: "A baby grows in a mother's belly and comes out when he or she is ready." This will satisfy their curiosity for a while.

The next step may be to say: "The mom and dad make a baby. God takes a little part from the mom and a little part from the dad and makes a baby. The baby grows in the mom's womb and the baby comes out of the mom's vagina when he or she is ready."

Eventually, they will want to know how the baby gets in the mother's uterus. It is important to answer clearly while still being age-appropriate in your explanation of sexual intercourse. Of course, not all babies are made this way. If your child was made in a different way, such as IVF, you can choose to add in how they were made, or you can wait until they ask how they were made.

It is helpful for children to understand that some people have babies and some do not. Sometimes that is their choice and sometimes they cannot make a baby. Regardless of how your child was made—typical pregnancy, IVF, or adoption—it could be very powerful for them to hear why you decided to become a parent and that the Bible says "Children are a gift from the Lord" (Psalm 127:3 NIrV). There is great comfort in a child knowing that God made them and has planned each day of their life.

We want to be clear that it is up to you to decide how much detail you want to provide and when. This should be based on the conversations you have already had with your child and what you think your child is ready to understand.

When you are asked "the question," remember a few things:

1 Emphasize God's love and care.

Your child's question is an opportunity to share how they were "wonderfully made" by our amazing, creative God and that God planned for them to be here (Psalm 139:14 NIV). Each person is made in the image of God, which shapes how we think about ourselves and others. One of our other children's books, *God Made Me in His Image*, would be helpful here. What a great thing to tell a child: "God made you on purpose because he wanted you in his world." He planned for each baby to be born and celebrates each birth. In doing this, you make God's love, care, and the miracle of his gift of life front and center.

2 Determine the context.

Since it is a conversation, ask questions. Your child's answer may provide context for their question and help you know how to focus your response. Did they hear something at school? Did they see a pregnant woman? Did they read something in a book?

3 Ask what they think.

Asking your child what they think can be a fruitful launching point for a more helpful discussion.

4 Keep your response simple and short.

Sometimes a few sentences are all that's needed. Often the simplest explanation is sufficient. Keep it simple and then see if they have any follow-up questions. If they want more information, they will let you know—now or later.

5 Find ways to make the conversations natural and normal.

Find ways to talk about this subject while eating dinner, taking a walk, visiting the zoo, out for a drive, etc. If the conversations are natural and normal, that will help your child feel comfortable with other questions or concerns that arise. This is exactly what we hope for as parents.

6 Don't ignore the question.

Redirecting or ignoring the question will not make your child's curiosity go away. It will only communicate that they should not come to you with their questions. They will likely ask someone else.

7 Don't make it weird.

Young children do not know that asking where babies come from can be awkward for you. For them, asking about reproduction is no different from asking any other question. Try to be casual and straightforward in your response. *How* you respond communicates just as much as *what* you say. Try to stay calm and not reveal shock, embarrassment, concern, or frustration. Your discomfort may make your child feel shame for asking a normal question.

8 Proper names for private parts.

This conversation is an opportunity to teach your child the proper names of body parts related to reproduction. Focus on the parts they can see—like the penis and vagina. One of our other children's books, *God Made All of Me*, would be helpful here.

9 Use correct language and define terms.

Using accurate terms for body parts can avoid unnecessary confusion. For example, babies grow in the uterus or womb. If you use terms like "stomach" or "tummy," it can be confusing since that is where food goes. Explain any words your child does not know. This keeps them from feeling overwhelmed with information and it helps keep the conversation from feeling abstract.

10 Make sure they understand what you are saying.

Check their understanding and encourage more discussion by asking, "Does that answer your question?" or, "Is there anything else you want to know?"

Dedicated to our niece, Luna.
We are so grateful that God made you.

New Growth Press, Greensboro, NC 27401
Text Copyright © 2022 by Lindsey A. Holcomb and Justin S. Holcomb
Illustration Copyright © 2022 by Trish Mahoney

Art and Design: Trish Mahoney

ISBN: 978-1-64507-223-2

Library of Congress Cataloging-in-Publication Data on file
LCCN 2022011370

Printed in India

29 28 27 26 25 24 23 22   1 2 3 4 5